EASY COIN TRICKS

WITHDRAWN

Stephanie Turnbull

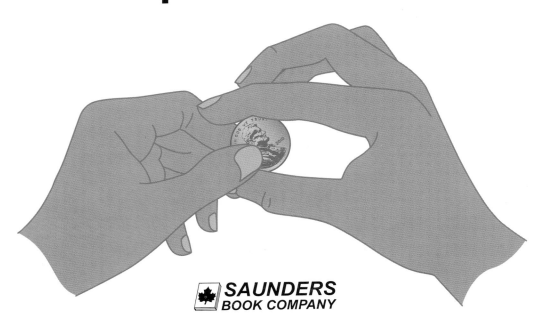

SAUNDERS
BOOK COMPANY

Published by Saunders Book Company
27 Stewart Road, Collingwood, ON Canada L9Y 4M7

Printed in the United States of America, at Corporate Graphics
in North Mankato, Minnesota.

Created by Appleseed Editions, Ltd.
Designed and illustrated by Guy Callaby
Edited by Mary-Jane Wilkins

Library of Congress Cataloging-in-Publication Data

Turnbull, Stephanie.
Easy Coin tricks / Stephanie Turnbull.
    pages cm. -- (Beginner magic)
Includes index.
ISBN 978-1-77092-155-9 (paperback)
1. Coin tricks--Juvenile literature. I. Title.
GV1559.T86 2014
793.8--dc23
                        2012051824

Photo acknowledgements
page 2 iStockphoto/Thinkstock;
4 Hemera/Thinkstock, 5 eAlisa/Shutterstock
Front cover: Getty Images/Thinkstock,
iStockphoto/Thinkstock

DAD0508
052013
9 8 7 6 5 4 3 2 1

Contents

Amazing Money Magic

Great magicians always have a few coin tricks up their sleeves. Why not learn some yourself? Coins are easy to carry around, so you can surprise friends with a quick trick whenever you have a spare moment!

Tips and Ideas
Look out for these boxes. They're full of handy tips for making tricks work perfectly.

Smooth moves
Magic tricks usually involve a sneaky move or two, so it's important to practice well before you perform. Collect a few coins and get used to handling them. Small coins are very useful as you can hide them in your hand easily.

head

tail

Coins have a head on one side but not on the other (the tail). This is important in some tricks.

Talking Heads

This is a great coin trick that doesn't need fancy finger work—just a good memory and quick thinking!

1. Ask a friend to put a few coins on the table. Quickly count the number of heads. Remember whether this is an odd or even number.

There is an ODD number of heads.

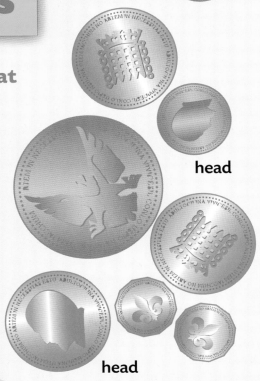

head

head

head

2. Turn away and ask your friend to turn over any TWO coins. Ask them to do this a few times.

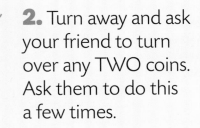

They must turn two coins every time.

3. Ask them to cover one coin. Say, *"Did you know I can talk to coins? They always tell me which way up they are!"*

As you talk, quickly look at the coins and count the heads again.

There is now an EVEN number of heads.

If the number of heads is still odd or still even, then the hidden coin is TAIL up.

If it's changed, then the coin is HEADS up.

4. Pretend to listen to the coin under your friend's hand, then say whether its head or tail is on top.

I can hear the coin loud and clear... it's definitely heads up!

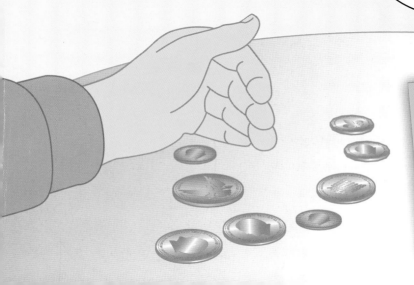

Do this a few times to prove it wasn't a lucky guess! Add more coins or use different ones.

Money Mind-Reader

This trick needs some planning —but then it's easy.

1. Find ten coins that are all different in some way: different values, country of origin, design, or date.

2. Put them in a bag and place it in the fridge for a few minutes, so the coins are cool – but not freezing cold!

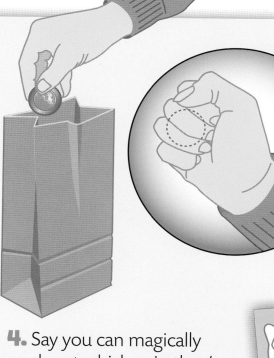

3. Now ask a friend to pick out a coin from the bag. Tell them to look at it carefully, without showing you, then keep it hidden in their hand.

4. Say you can magically work out which coin they're holding. Stare at them as if you're reading their mind.

Don't do this trick twice—it won't work the second time!

5. Ask your friend to put the coin back in the bag, shake it and hand it to you. Quickly feel around in the bag. Their coin will be warmer than the rest. Pull it out and show it!

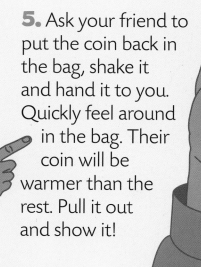

Coin Squeeze

For this quick, fun trick you need paper, a pencil, and scissors.

1. Draw around a small coin, such as a dime, on a piece of paper.

2. Carefully cut out the circle to make a hole in the paper.

3. Fold the paper across the middle of the hole. Drop the coin inside the fold to show that it falls straight through the hole.

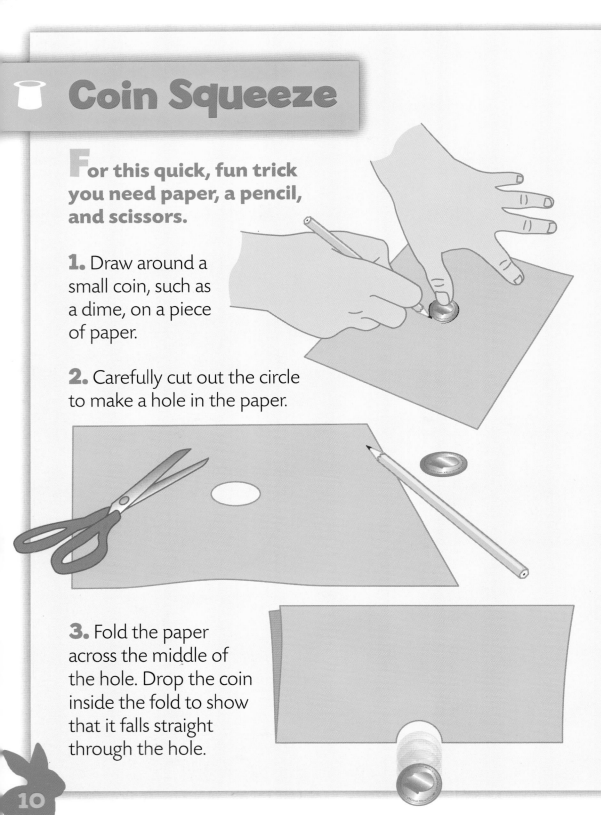

4. Now put a big coin into the fold, such as a quarter. Of course it won't fall through because it's too big. Say that you can make it squeeze through the hole.

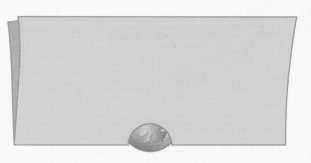

5. Pretend to concentrate hard. Holding the paper by the fold, quickly push the sides up and into the middle. The paper bulges out – and the coin slips through the hole.

The faster you do step 5, the better the trick looks— so get practicing!

6. Unfold the paper to prove that you didn't rip the paper or alter the hole!

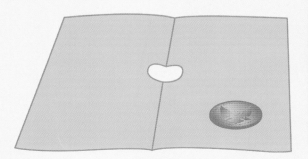

Magic Secrets

Some magicians pretend to bend coins by magic. They may use flexible coins, or sneakily swap a real coin for a bent one.

Disappearing Coin

The secret of this trick is simple—glue! Use a small coin such as a dime, and don't let your friend hold it afterwards, or they'll notice it's sticky.

1. Just before you do the trick, secretly smear glue on the back of one hand.

2. Take a coin in the other hand and show it to a friend. Show them that your other hand is empty.

glue

Magic Secrets

Magicians sometimes use clear tape to make small objects stick —or very thin thread to make them seem to float.

3. Grip the coin in your thumb and first two fingers. Hold up your other hand in a fist and pretend to push the coin inside.

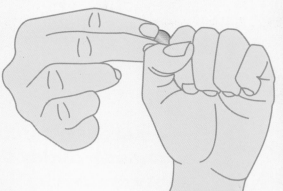

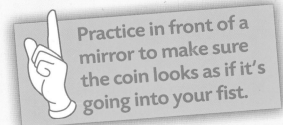

This is what you see.

4. Here's the sneaky move: push the two fingers into your fist and use your thumb to slide the coin onto the back of your hand. Press it on the sticky patch.

5. Open your fingers and show that your hand is empty. Now say magic words or blow on your other fist, then open it to show that the coin has disappeared.

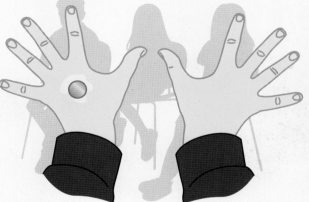

Don't turn your hands and show the coin!

6. To make the coin reappear, close your fist again and do step 4 in reverse—use your thumb and two fingers to slide the coin back into your non-sticky hand.

Practice in front of a mirror to make sure the coin looks as if it's going into your fist.

13

Magical Moving Coins

Learn to move coins around in your hands so quickly that no one notices.

1. Put a quarter in the middle of your left palm and a penny on the right side of your right palm. Rest your hands flat on a table and show the coins to a friend.

2. Quickly turn over your hands so they're face down on the table. The penny should flip across so that it ends up under your left hand with the quarter.

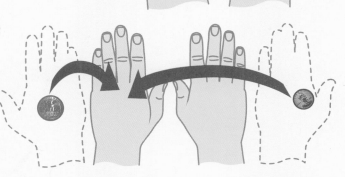

This takes practice but it does work!

3. Ask your friend to remember which coin was in which hand—then lift your hands to show them they're wrong!

4. Say you'll let them try again. Place the penny on the right side of your right palm again, but this time put the quarter on the left side of your left palm.

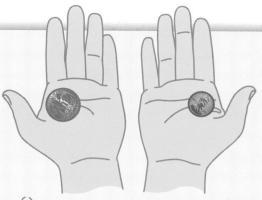

5. Now slap both hands over again. This time, each coin should jump to the other hand.

6. Ask your friend which coin was in which hand—then show them they're wrong again!

Magic Secrets

Coin magicians use their fingers to flick, roll, twirl, and balance coins.

Try doing this on a tablecloth or placemat to help you control the coins better.

Coin-Eating Hanky

For this trick you need a large hanky or scarf and a shirt or jacket with a top pocket.

1. Show a friend the coin and hanky, then hold them in front of you. Hold the coin with the fingers of your left hand and one corner of the hanky in your right.

Meet my amazing coin-eating hanky!

If you're using a shirt pocket, make sure the coin can't be seen through the material.

2. Hold the coin at the level of your pocket. Drape the hanky over the coin and pull it toward you, keeping your left hand still.

pocket

3. Keep pulling the hanky until it comes off the coin, to show the coin is still in your left hand. Your right hand should now be touching your pocket.

Oh... perhaps he's not hungry.

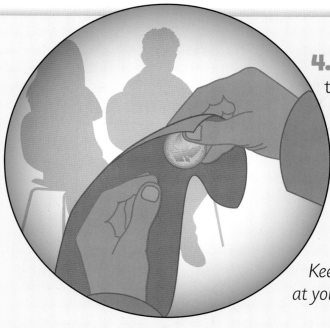

4. Drape the hanky over the coin again as if to repeat steps 2 and 3 —but this time, secretly grip the coin with your right thumb.

Keep looking at your left hand!

5. Pull the hanky toward you again. Keep your left fingers upright as if they're still holding the coin. When your right hand reaches your pocket, drop the coin in it.

Coin drops into pocket.

You see? He ate it all up!

6. As the hanky comes off your left hand, your friend will see the coin is gone! Show both hands and shake the hanky to prove it's empty.

Clever Coin Throw

This trick uses a coin move called a French drop. It takes practice, but works well.

1. Hold a coin in your right hand between your thumb and first finger.

2. Put your left hand over the coin as if you're going to pass it to that hand...

... but let the coin drop into your right hand instead. Quickly make a fist with the left hand as if the coin is inside.

3. Hold up your left fist. Keep the fingers of your right hand loosely curled around the coin to hide it. This is called a palm.

4. Pretend to throw the coin up and toward your friend, opening your fist to show it's now empty. Pretend to look for the coin.

Focus on the fist and ignore the other hand—then your friend will, too!

If this is too tricky, sneakily drop the coin into your lap or pocket in step 3, then open your fist to show the coin has disappeared.

5. While your friend looks too, quickly reach your right hand to their ear and push the coin into your fingers. Show it to your friend. It looks as if you just plucked it from their ear!

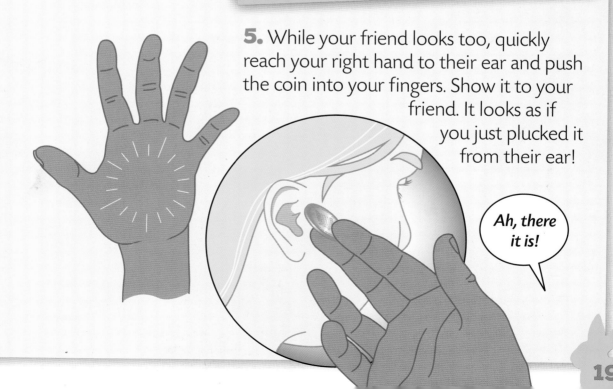

Ah, there it is!

19

Ripped-Up Coin

Here's another trick that involves hiding a coin in your hand.

1. Cut a piece of paper 4 inches (10 cm) square, then fold it so one side is about 1 inch (2.5 cm) shorter than the other. As you do this, ask your friend for a quarter. Drop it into the fold.

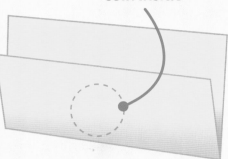

coin inside

Keep the shorter side facing you.

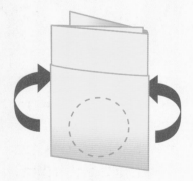

your view

2. Hold up the paper and fold both sides back behind the coin.

3. Next, fold the top flap down away from you. It looks as if you've sealed the top of the packet— but there's an opening.

4. Hold the packet at the open end and ask your friend to feel the coin.

opening faces you

friend's hand

5. Now turn your hand so the opening faces down. Let the coin slide into your hand as you grab the packet with your other hand.

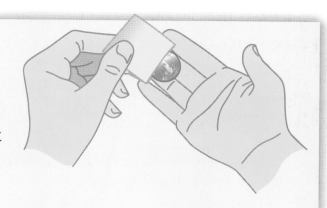

6. Grip the coin gently with your middle fingers. Let the other fingers curl a bit, too, and hold your hand naturally.

This is called a finger palm.

Practice palming while you're out and about to get comfortable doing it.

7. Using the first finger and thumb of each hand, tear up the packet and throw the pieces in the air.

8. While your friend is looking at the bits of paper and wondering where their coin has gone, pluck it from their ear as shown on page 19, or sneak it into your pocket. But give it back later or your friends may start disappearing, too!

Magic Words

French drop
A way of making a coin vanish. A magician seems to pass the coin from one hand to another, but really lets it drop into the first hand. It works best if it is done quickly and casually.

head
The side of a coin that usually shows a person's head.

mentalist
A magician who pretends to make magical things happen using mind power.

palm
The flat front of your hand. In magic, a palm also means a way of gripping something small in your palm so that your hand looks empty from the other side.

patter
Words a magician speaks while performing. Patter needs to be worked out and practiced as part of a trick. Often it helps distract attention from sneaky moves!

tail
The side of a coin that doesn't show a person's head.

Magic Web Sites

To learn more about coin magic and try more coin tricks, visit these helpful web sites:

www.birthday-party-magician.com/easy-coin-trick.html

http://magic.about.com/od/Easy-Magic-Tricks-for-Kids/tp/Easy-Magic-Tricks-For-Kids-With-Coins.htm

www.freemagictricks4u.com/free-coin-tricks.html

Index

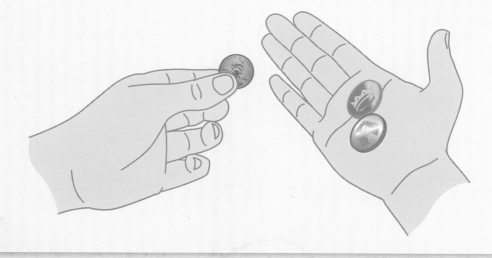